Printed in Great Britain
by Amazon

70831881R00059